REDSTONE STICKER BOOK

First published in Great Britain 2026 by Farshore
An imprint of HarperCollins*Publishers*, 1 London Bridge Street, London SE1 9GF
www.farshore.co.uk

HarperCollins*Publishers*, Macken House, 39/40 Mayor Street Upper, Dublin 1, D01 C9W8, Ireland

Special thanks to Alex Wiltshire, Sherin Kwan, Lauren Marklund, Kelsey Ranallo and Milo Bengtsson

© 2026 Mojang AB. All Rights Reserved. Minecraft, the Minecraft logo, the Mojang Studios logo
and the Creeper logo are trademarks of the Microsoft group of companies.

MOJANG STUDIOS

ISBN 978 0 00 873312 4
Printed in Poland
001

A CIP catalogue record for this title is available from the British Library.

All rights reserved.

Without limiting the exclusive rights of any author, contributor or the publisher of this publication, any unauthorised use of this publication to train generative artificial intelligence (AI) technologies is expressly prohibited. HarperCollins also exercise their rights under Article 4(3) of the Digital Single Market Directive 2019/790 and expressly reserve this publication from the text and data mining exception.

ONLINE SAFETY FOR YOUNGER FANS

Spending time online is great fun! Here are a few simple rules to help younger fans stay safe and keep the internet a great place to spend time:
- Never give out your real name – don't use it as your username.
- Never give out any of your personal details.
- Never tell anybody which school you go to or how old you are.
- Never tell anybody your password except a parent or a guardian.
- Be aware that you must be 13 or over to create an account on many sites. Always check the site policy and ask a parent or guardian for permission before registering.
- Always tell a parent or guardian if something is worrying you.

Stay safe online. Any website addresses listed in this book are correct at the time of going to print. However, Farshore is not responsible for content hosted by third parties. Please be aware that online content can be subject to change and websites can contain content that is unsuitable for children. We advise that all children are supervised when using the internet.

This book contains FSC™ certified paper and other controlled
sources to ensure responsible forest management.

For more information visit: www.harpercollins.co.uk/green

LET'S GO

On every page, place a redstone sticker once you've finished the build!

Ready for a thrilling redstone quest? Of course you are – that's why you're here! But before you sprint off on your adventures, it's time to start crafting.

Use your stickers to equip your friends with their armour and tools. Then find the right stickers to complete the crafting recipes to make redstone items. Finish by decorating with your extra stickers!

BLOCK OF REDSTONE

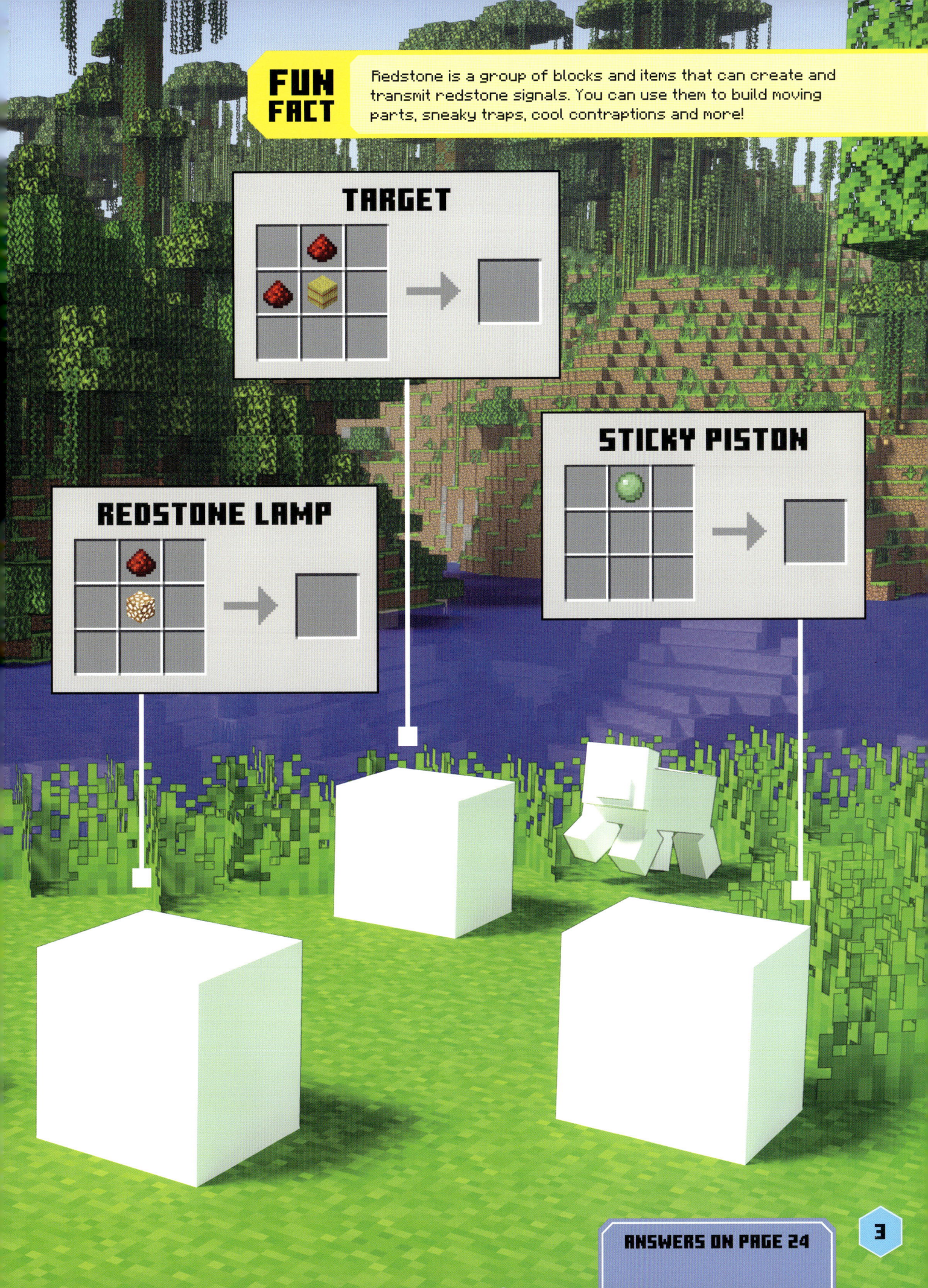

LIGHT IT UP!

PAGE COMPLETED

Let's start by checking out your base. Nice, right? But something's missing. Here's a bright idea, try adding cool lights so you can see what you're doing!

Find your stickers to light up the lamps. Then choose where you'd like to place the rest of your bright and colourful stickers in the scene!

Before you start your redstone builds, stick the correct item in your inventory slots to begin!

STICK HERE

REDSTONE LAYOUTS

In most of these builds, you'll need to lay a trail of redstone dust to complete your layouts. A redstone layout glows red when it's transmitting a signal. If it's dull, it isn't active.

FUN FACT

A redstone layout means a build, such as a trap or a moving contraption, that is made up of redstone blocks and items. The build works by transmitting redstone signals.

4

BLOCK OF REDSTONE

This block creates a constant redstone signal and can't be deactivated. It'll help stop zombies and other horrid hostile mobs from spawning inside the base to say hi ... or arghhh!

STICK HERE

REDSTONE LAMP

Once you've placed the lamp next to your redstone dust, it will activate instantly. De-light-ful work!

STICK HERE

AUTOMATIC DOORS

PAGE COMPLETED

Yikes! Night has arrived already and hostile mobs have spawned nearby. Your base isn't safe until you finish building a secure door. Away, zombies, away!

Grab your stickers to reveal some fun facts about the mobs! Then add a button and a trail of redstone dust to complete the layouts.

MOB WATCH

Use your stickers to match the mobs with their fun facts.

SKELETON
STICK HERE

SPIDER
STICK HERE

ZOMBIE
STICK HERE

6 — ANSWERS ON PAGE 24

SUPER STAIRCASE

Now it's light again, give your base entrance an upgrade. A redstone genius doesn't just hop and jump to get in, so build a staircase to get there in style!

To create an automatic staircase, use the sticky piston, redstone dust and pressure plate stickers. Decorate the scene, and race up the stairs!

REDSTONE DUST

Lay a trail of redstone dust along and over the blocks, connecting the sticky piston and pressure plate.

SPEEDY SEARCH

Look around the area for these hidden items and stick a tick once you've found them!

- Redstone lamp
- Chicken jockey
- Bamboo mosaic block
- Creeper

ANSWERS ON PAGE 24

STICKY PISTON

Sticky pistons are great for moving mechanisms. When activated, they will push a block out. When deactivated, they'll pull the block back to its original position.

PRESSURE PLATE

When you stand on the plate, it will push the staircase out, but be quick when running up the stairs! The steps will pull back in soon after you step off the plate. Ready? Start running!

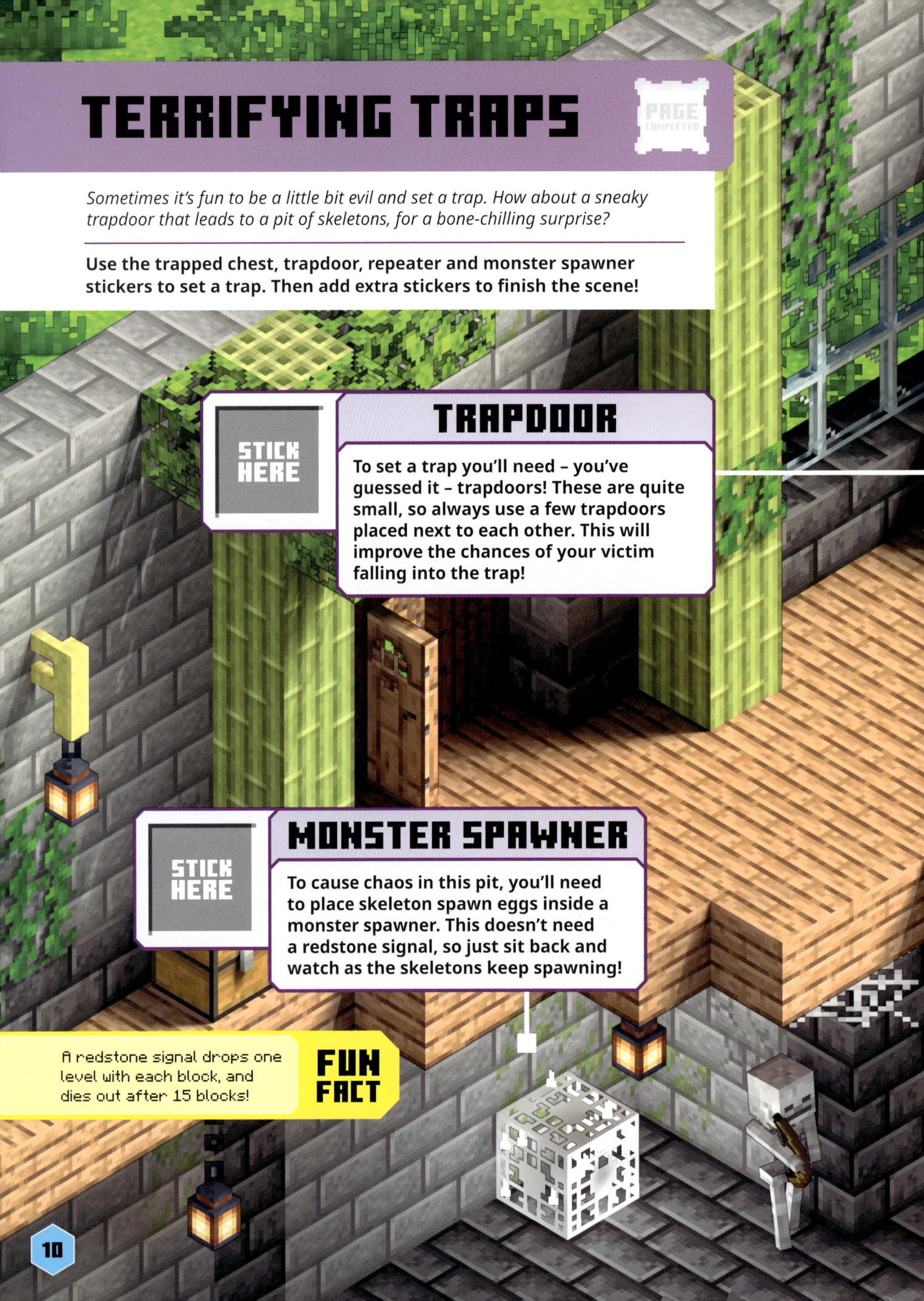

TERRIFYING TRAPS

PAGE COMPLETED

Sometimes it's fun to be a little bit evil and set a trap. How about a sneaky trapdoor that leads to a pit of skeletons, for a bone-chilling surprise?

Use the trapped chest, trapdoor, repeater and monster spawner stickers to set a trap. Then add extra stickers to finish the scene!

TRAPDOOR

STICK HERE

To set a trap you'll need – you've guessed it – trapdoors! These are quite small, so always use a few trapdoors placed next to each other. This will improve the chances of your victim falling into the trap!

MONSTER SPAWNER

STICK HERE

To cause chaos in this pit, you'll need to place skeleton spawn eggs inside a monster spawner. This doesn't need a redstone signal, so just sit back and watch as the skeletons keep spawning!

FUN FACT

A redstone signal drops one level with each block, and dies out after 15 blocks!

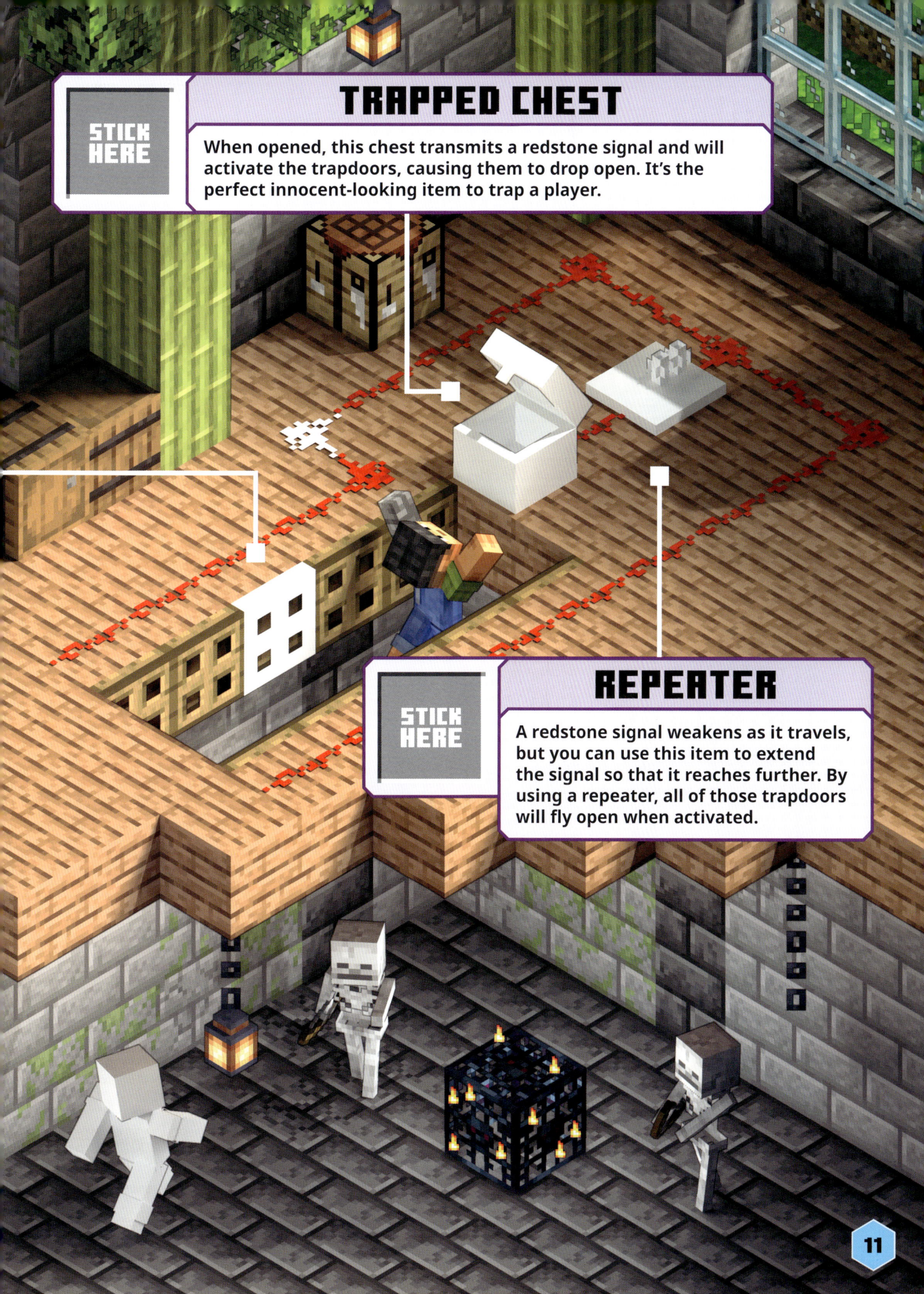

TRAPPED CHEST

When opened, this chest transmits a redstone signal and will activate the trapdoors, causing them to drop open. It's the perfect innocent-looking item to trap a player.

REPEATER

A redstone signal weakens as it travels, but you can use this item to extend the signal so that it reaches further. By using a repeater, all of those trapdoors will fly open when activated.

REDSTONE RAILS

You've mined deep underground, so whilst you're here you might as well build your own railroad. You and the mobs are about to go on a wild ride!

Stick on powered rails and a redstone torch to complete your redstone layouts. Then stick the minecarts and finishing touches to the scene!

REDSTONE TORCH

For powered rails to work, they need a redstone signal to activate them. Redstone torches are great because they produce a constant signal. You could also use buttons, blocks of redstone or pressure plates!

STICK HERE

POWERED RAILS

When activated, powered rails will push a minecart along. They can be placed uphill, downhill or just in a straight line. If the tracks are glowing red, it means they're active.

STICK HERE

12

INTRUDER ALERT

You've returned to your base to stash the ores you mined and ... What?! Your house has been looted! Did you leave the door open? It's time to build an alarm.

Find the note block, repeater and tripwire hook stickers to create an intruder alarm to alert you of thieves. Then decorate the scene!

NOTE BLOCK

Note blocks create sounds when activated with a redstone signal. You can place a note block on top of other blocks to sound like musical instruments, such as sand for a drum or hay for a banjo!

MUSIC MYSTERY

Use your stickers to play your intruder alarm in this sudoku! Each row, column and little rectangle should have one of each item.

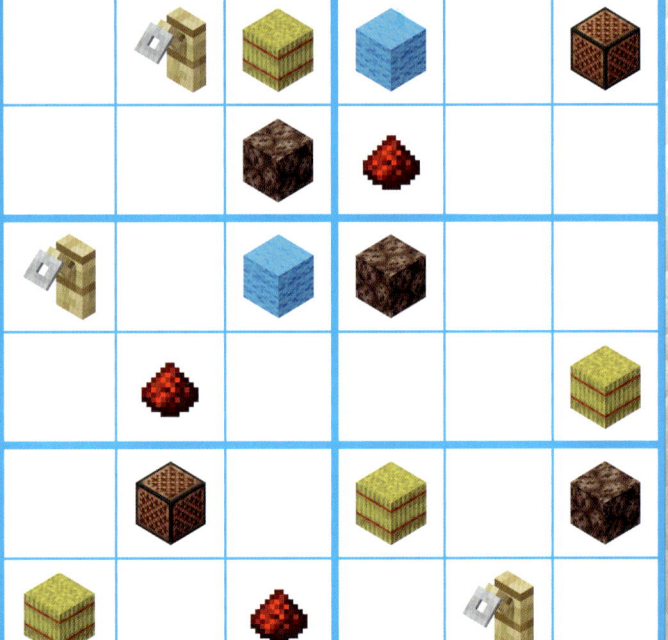

ANSWERS ON PAGE 24

BELL

To make a tip-top alarm, you'll need a big bell. Luckily for you, every village has one.

STICK HERE

REDSTONE DUST

Lay a trail of redstone dust, connecting the bell and daylight detector. As soon as it's morning, the daylight detector will activate the bell to ring ... very, very loudly!

STICK HERE

TNT TIME

PAGE COMPLETED

These villagers really need a fancier place to live. Perhaps you should build them a better home? But before that, you need to make some more room ...

Use the TNT, target and bow stickers to create a controlled demolition to get rid of the mountains for a mind-blowing upgrade!

REDSTONE DUST

Use a trail of redstone dust to connect the target and the TNT blocks.

STICK HERE

BOW AND ARROW

You'll need to fire the arrow directly at the target to activate the signal and make the TNT blocks explode. So it's time to aim and fire!

STICK HERE

TNT

When activated, TNT takes a few seconds to explode, like a creeper! This gives you enough time to run away and take cover.

TARGET

When a target is hit by an item, such as an arrow, it transmits a temporary redstone signal and activates the TNT blocks. Say goodbye to the mountains!

STICK HERE

FIREWORK NIGHT

It's time to celebrate all of your amazing creations! What better way to do this than by making a firework show for yourself and the villagers?

Grab your dispenser and lightning rod stickers to finish this colourful scene. Remember to add extra stickers of your captivated audience!

LIGHTNING ROD

Lightning rods redirect lightning strikes in a storm to a specific spot. When struck, they transmit a redstone signal. Just remember, you'll always need a thunderstorm for this to work!

STICK HERE

CRACKLING CONUNDRUMS

Use your stickers to complete the sequences so you can create more fireworks!

ANSWERS ON PAGE 24

DISPENSER

Dispensers release items in their storage slots when they receive a redstone signal. When activated and loaded up with lots of firework rockets, the dispensers will shoot these into the sky to create fireworks!

STICK HERE

THE BIG FINALE

You've reached the end of your redstone journey! Now it's time to prove that you are a true redstone genius with a quickfire sticker quiz. 3, 2, 1, go!

Can you remember all the redstone blocks and components that you used? Use your stickers to label them in the scene below.

1: STICK HERE
2: STICK HERE
3: STICK HERE

ANSWERS ON PAGE 24

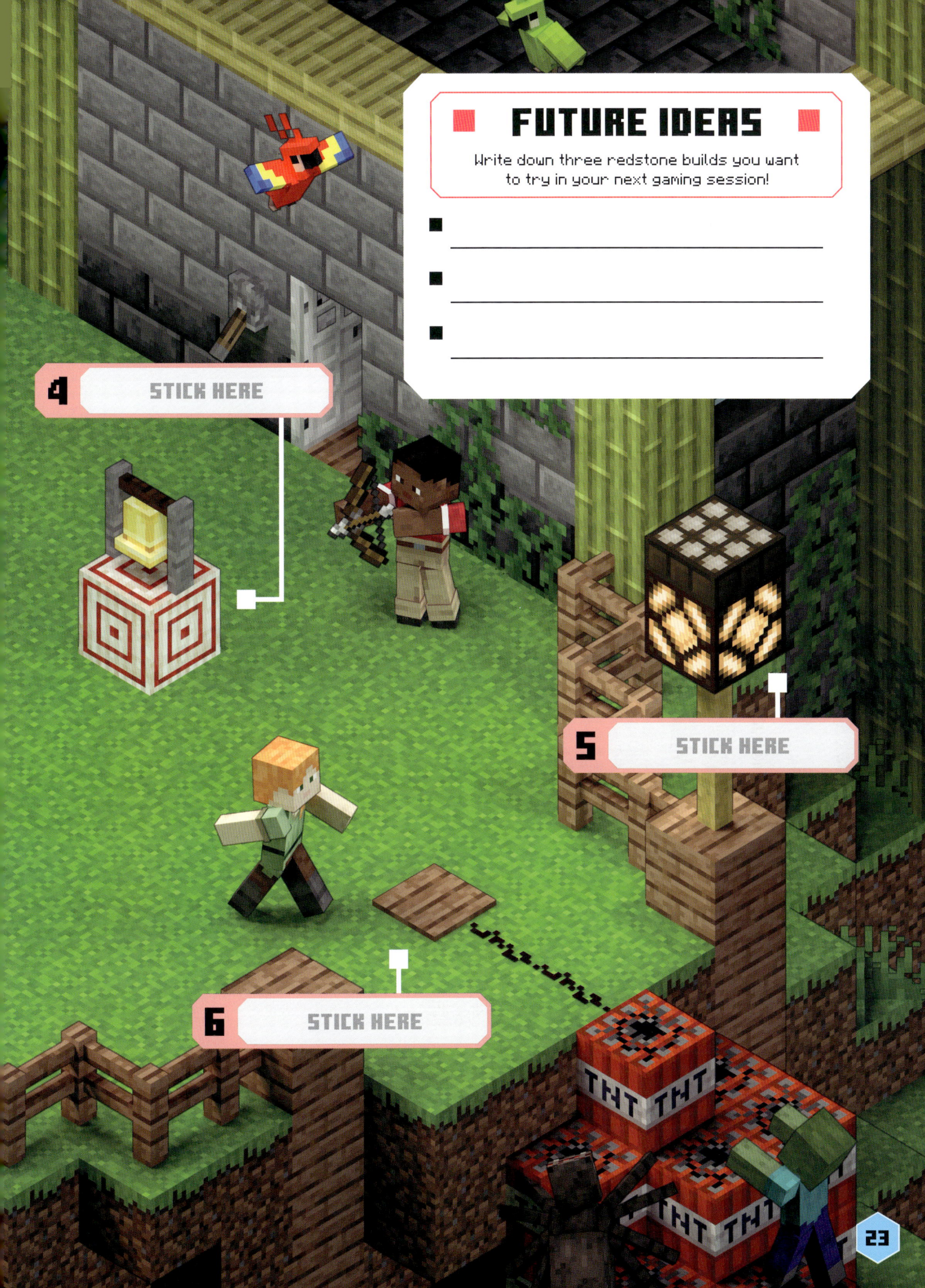

FUTURE IDEAS
Write down three redstone builds you want to try in your next gaming session!

- _____
- _____
- _____

ANSWERS

Your redstone adventure is now complete! How did you do? Check out the answers below to see!

PAGES 2-3

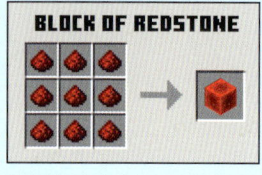 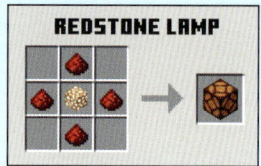 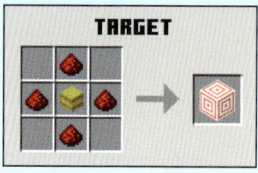 

PAGES 6-7

SKELETON - When defeated, this mob drops bones, or even a skull if a charged creeper is involved!

SPIDER - This mob only turns hostile in the dark.

ZOMBIE - This mob tends to overwhelm players in groups. Watch out!

PAGES 8-9

PAGES 14-15

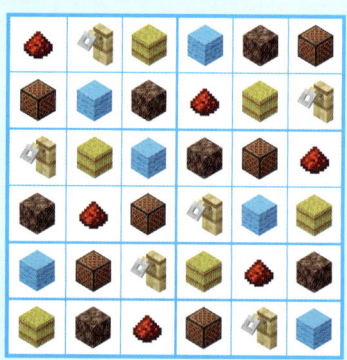

PAGES 20-21

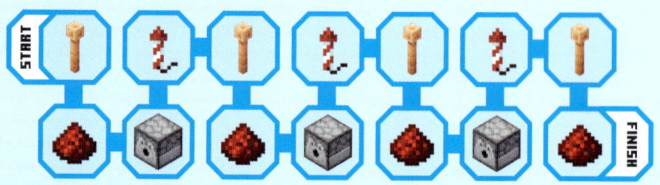

PAGES 22-23

1 - Powered rails
2 - Daylight detector
3 - Block of redstone
4 - Target
5 - Redstone lamp
6 - Pressure plate

LET'S GO P2-3

LIGHT IT UP! P4-5

AUTOMATIC DOORS P6-7

When defeated, this mob drops bones, or even a skull if a charged creeper is involved!

This mob only turns hostile in the dark.

This mob tends to overwhelm players in groups. Watch out!

SUPER STAIRCASE P8-9

EXTRA STICKERS FOR FUN!

TERRIFYING TRAPS P10-11

REDSTONE RAILS P12-13

INTRUDER ALERT   P14-15

RISE AND SHINE   P16-17
PART 1

RISE AND SHINE P16-17
PART 2

TNT TIME P18-19

FIREWORK NIGHT P20-21
PART 1

FIREWORK NIGHT P20-21
PART 2

THE BIG FINALE P22-23

| BLOCK OF REDSTONE | DAYLIGHT DETECTOR | POWERED RAILS |
| TARGET | REDSTONE LAMP | PRESSURE PLATE |

EXTRA STICKERS FOR FUN!

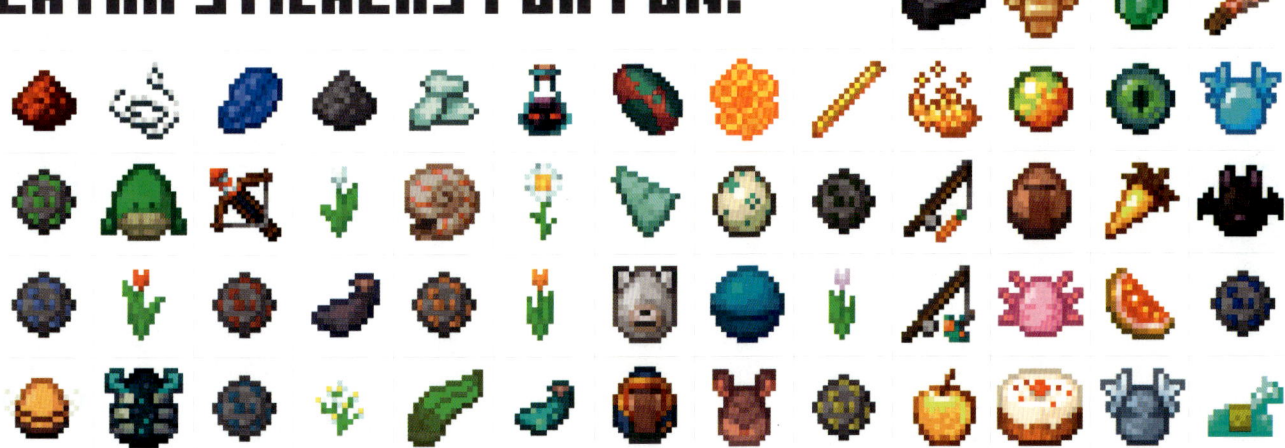

COMPLETED IT STICKERS!